Facts About the Skunk

By Lisa Strattin

© 2019 Lisa Strattin

FREE BOOK

FREE FOR ALL SUBSCRIBERS

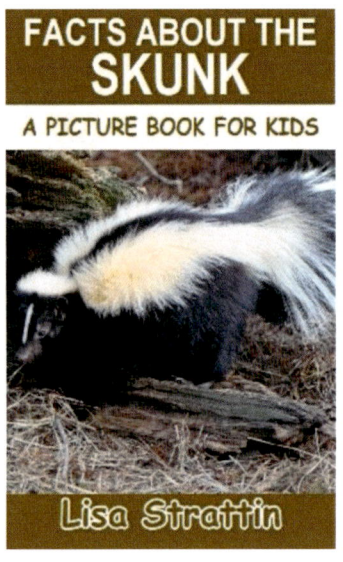

LisaStrattin.com/Subscribe-Here

BOX SET

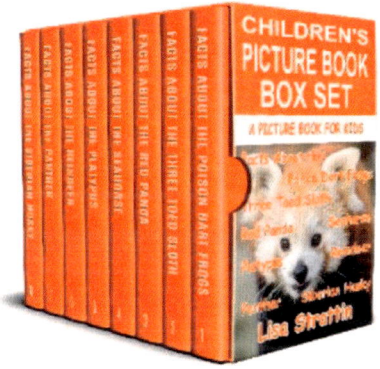

- **FACTS ABOUT THE POISON DART FROGS**
- **FACTS ABOUT THE THREE TOED SLOTH**
  - **FACTS ABOUT THE RED PANDA**
  - **FACTS ABOUT THE SEAHORSE**
  - **FACTS ABOUT THE PLATYPUS**
  - **FACTS ABOUT THE REINDEER**
  - **FACTS ABOUT THE PANTHER**
- **FACTS ABOUT THE SIBERIAN HUSKY**

LisaStrattin.com/BookBundle

Facts for Kids Picture Books by Lisa Strattin

Little Blue Penguin, Vol 92

Chipmunk, Vol 5

Frilled Lizard, Vol 39

Blue and Gold Macaw, Vol 13

Poison Dart Frogs, Vol 50

Blue Tarantula, Vol 115

African Elephants, Vol 8

Amur Leopard, Vol 89

Sabre Tooth Tiger, Vol 167

Baboon, Vol 174

Sign Up for New Release Emails Here

LisaStrattin.com/subscribe-here

All rights reserved. No part of this book may be reproduced by any means whatsoever without the written permission from the author, except brief portions quoted for purpose of review.

All information in this book has been carefully researched and checked for factual accuracy. However, the author and publisher makes no warranty, express or implied, that the information contained herein is appropriate for every individual, situation or purpose and assume no responsibility for errors or omissions. The reader assumes the risk and full responsibility for all actions, and the author will not be held responsible for any loss or damage, whether consequential, incidental, special or otherwise, that may result from the information presented in this book.

All images are free for use or purchased from stock photo sites or royalty free for commercial use.

Some coloring pages might be of the general species due to lack of available images.

I have relied on my own observations as well as many different sources for this book and I have done my best to check facts and give credit where it is due. In the event that any material is used without proper permission, please contact me so that the oversight can be corrected.

COVER IMAGE

By http://www.birdphotos.com - Own work, CC BY 3.0, https://commons.wikimedia.org/w/index.php?curid=4409510

ADDITIONAL IMAGES

https://www.flickr.com/photos/gregthebusker/5889825633/

https://www.flickr.com/photos/santamonicamtns/9098637674/

https://www.flickr.com/photos/boviate/4952766119/

https://www.flickr.com/photos/gamppart/7391196102/

https://www.flickr.com/photos/widnr/6511386457/

https://www.flickr.com/photos/lblkytn/14928066475/

https://www.flickr.com/photos/gotovan/7177526559/

https://www.flickr.com/photos/28122162@N04/5982866012/

https://www.flickr.com/photos/jcapaldi/8570741286/

https://www.flickr.com/photos/tambako/9895994103/

Contents

INTRODUCTION	9
CHARACTERISTICS	11
APPEARANCE	13
REPRODUCTION	15
LIFE SPAN	17
SIZE	19
HABITAT	21
DIET	23
ENEMIES	25
SUITABILITY AS PETS	27

INTRODUCTION

The skunk, also known as the polecat, is most commonly known for their ability to secrete a foul, strong smelling odor from their rear end, when the skunk feels that it is threatened.

CHARACTERISTICS

There are 11 known species of skunk in the world, with most of them living on the American continent. Two of these species are found in Indonesia and the Philippines.

Although skunks have excellent smell and hearing, skunks are known to have very poor vision and can only see objects that are right in front of them. With the introduction of cars, numerous skunks have been killed on the roads as the skunks cannot see the cars coming towards them until it is too late.

APPEARANCE

The color of the skunk can vary from the typical black and white to grey, cream and even brown. However, all skunks are striped and baby skunks are even born with their striped markings regardless of their color.

REPRODUCTION

Baby skunks are born blind and without any teeth. They don't open their eyes until they are a few weeks old. The baby skunks are also unable to use their defensive spray when they are first born. The skunks spraying ability develops just before it's eyes open when the skunk is a couple of weeks old.

Female skunks usually give birth to their babies in the hotter month of May after a gestation period of a couple of months. The female skunk digs out a burrow in which to give birth to her skunk babies (called kits) and the babies will usually stay with their mother until they are about a year old and are old enough to mate themselves.

LIFE SPAN

Generally, skunks can live for 5 to 8 years, in the appropriate habitat, as long as they are safe from road traffic.

SIZE

The average skunk is between 16 and 28 inches in length and weighs about the same as a house cat.

HABITAT

Skunks are generally solitary animals and only really come together to breed. In colder regions however, they have been known to inhabit communal burrows in order to try to keep each other warm. Most skunks hide in burrows during the day which the skunk digs out with its long front claws.

DIET

The skunk hunts insects, small birds and mammals. They also commonly eat berries, roots, grasses and fungi in order to supplement their diet.

ENEMIES

Most predators like wolves, foxes and badgers, seldom attack skunks, presumably out of fear of being sprayed. The exceptions are reckless predators whose attacks fail once they are sprayed. Dogs and the Great Horned Owl, are the skunk's only regular predator.

SUITABILITY AS PETS

Skunks have been kept as pets. In the case of wild skunks, the answer would be no. But domesticated skunks have been bred in captivity for over 60 years and are known to be quite docile and loving. They are easily trained to use a litter box just like a house cat.

You will need to locate a breeder in order to get one that is not from the wild that you could keep safely as a pet.

COLOR ME

COLOR ME

COLOR ME

COLOR ME

COLOR ME

COLOR ME

COLOR ME

COLOR ME

COLOR ME

COLOR ME

Please leave me a review here:

LisaStrattin.com/Review-Vol-262

For more Kindle Downloads Visit Lisa Strattin Author Page on Amazon Author Central

amazon.com/author/lisastrattin

To see upcoming titles, visit my website at LisaStrattin.com– most books available on Kindle!

LisaStrattin.com

FREE BOOK

FOR ALL SUBSCRIBERS – SIGN UP NOW

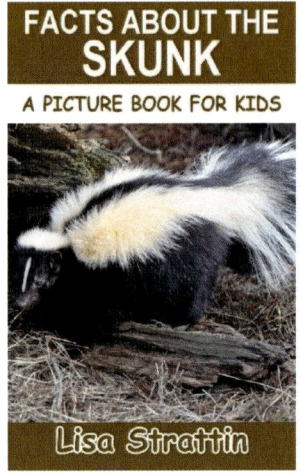

LisaStrattin.com/Subscribe-Here

LisaStrattin.com/Facebook

LisaStrattin.com/Youtube

Made in the USA
Monee, IL
07 December 2024